Focus on History

edited by Ray Mitchell and Geoffrey Middleton

At the Time of Geoffrey Chaucer

Jane Sayers

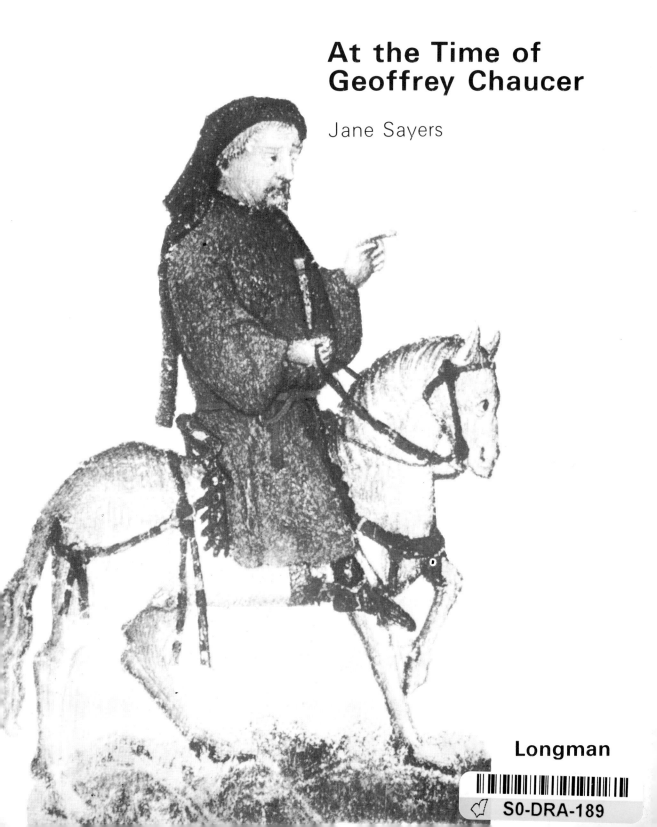

Longman

Who was Geoffrey Chaucer?

Chaucer as a boy

The man on the first page of this book is Geoffrey Chaucer. He was born in London in about 1340, more than 600 years ago. His father and grandfather were both wealthy wine merchants in Cheapside in the city of London, and so, because his father was a rich man, the young Geoffrey Chaucer was probably sent to school. There was a school at St Paul's cathedral at this time, where boys were taught to read, to write

and to count. The school would probably have looked much like this one. Notice the hard wooden benches the boys are sitting on.

Chaucer's father had a good business in the wine trade. Sailing vessels from Bordeaux in France brought red wine, called claret, into the port of London. White wines came by sea from Germany and sweet wines from as far away as Greece and Cyprus.

The London wine merchants were called vintners and most of them lived in the area of the city called Vintry, which was between Cheapside and the River Thames. They had formed themselves into a guild, or club, and in this club they controlled the trade in wine. They arranged for the buying and unloading of the wine and they decided at what price they would sell it. Only the members of the Vintners' Guild were allowed to sell wine in London. Wine was bought for every large household in the 14th century and so those who traded in wine were usually rich men.

A page in a noble household

When Chaucer left school, he was sent into the household of Elizabeth, Duchess of Clarence and Countess of Ulster. She was a daughter-in-law of King Edward III of England. The king, the dukes, the barons and the archbishops and bishops, all had households of several hundred people. The household of an important person had many departments—wardrobe (clothing), kitchen, pantry, buttery, poultry, scullery, chapel and a clerical staff.

As a page, Chaucer would have taken messages and waited at table. He would also have learnt how to behave politely and, as he grew older, how to draw up accounts and how to conduct business of all kinds.

Most noblemen and ladies liked house parties, hunting and tournaments, where knights jousted, or tried to unseat each other.

This picture shows a tournament, with grand lords and ladies of the household and their pages in the enclosure at the back.
Notice:
- the heavy armour the knights are wearing
- the symbol, or badge, on the helmets of the knights
- the tents where the knights prepared for the tournament.

When he was about 20, Chaucer left the household of the duchess for that of the king. He was now no longer a page but an 'esquire', or gentleman, in charge of the new pages and a household department. The business of the royal household included foreign affairs and missions abroad for the king, because then the royal household (and not parliament as it is today) was the centre of the nation's government. So in 1368 Chaucer was sent abroad on royal business by King Edward III.

The Customs' officer

About this time Chaucer married Philippa Roët, or as she is sometimes called, Philippa of the Pantry. She was a lady-in-waiting to the queen and later her sister married one of the king's sons, John of Gaunt. So Chaucer, though he was not of noble birth, was well known to some of the most important and powerful people in 14th century England.

This picture shows a gentleman, like Chaucer, talking to a lady in a garden. Find:
– the trellis with the roses growing up it
– the gentleman's dagger.

Now look carefully at their clothing and notice:
– the gentleman's cloak
– the lady's hat, or head-dress
– the belt she is holding in her hand
– the gentleman's socks. They are different colours.

During the 1370s Chaucer was kept busy by the king on foreign missions. Then in 1376 the king appointed Chaucer Comptroller of the Customs for the wool trade. Chaucer's job was to arrange for the collection of duties, or taxes, on all ships taking bales of wool out of England. These duties were collected in bags like this one and then sent to the king.

The Clerk of the Works

Chaucer's next job was as Clerk of the Works, looking after the royal palaces, castles and chapels, like the Tower of London, Westminster Palace, Windsor Castle and St George's Chapel. He had to arrange for repairs, see to the construction of new buildings, pay the workers, order the materials and so on. It was at this time that a lot of work was done for the king on Westminster Hall in the palace of Westminster.

The writer

Meanwhile, and probably from his late 20s, Chaucer had begun to write books. He was not just a powerful civil servant, or king's man of business, but he was also a learned man, who could speak French, Latin and Italian. By the 14th century most Londoners spoke English, not French, which was the language of the Court, nor Latin, which was the language of the Church. This was not the English that we use today, but a mixture of Norman-French and Anglo-Saxon. Here is Chaucer pointing to a poem which is written in 14th century English. See how many words you can recognise.

Chaucer's first work as a writer may have been a long poem called *The Book of the Duchess*. He then wrote *The Parliament of Birds*, but his most famous work was *The Canterbury Tales*, which was written probably in the 1380s. This book, which was written in verse, tells us about 14th century life and people.

Chaucer died in 1400. He had spent most of his life in London when he was not travelling abroad. He was the first great writer to write in English and one of the greatest storytellers of all time.

London in the 14th century

London was a very exciting city to live in. It had shops, streets, churches, chapels, gardens, a great bridge and warehouses and docks. There were about 35,000 people living there. It was the biggest city in England and one of the biggest in the world. But it was very crowded because the city was only $1\frac{1}{2}$ km square within the walls. Cities in the Middle Ages were walled to help defend them against attackers.

Ships came into the port of London bringing with them goods from across the world – silks, wine and gold. They sailed up the River Thames as far as London Bridge. London Bridge was said to be one of the wonders of the world. It had shops, houses and a chapel built on it.

The king and his court were often in London. They might stay at the White Tower in the Tower of London, which belonged to the king, and which you can see in the picture above. Notice:

– the White Tower, with the wall, towers and gateways round it
– London Bridge (at the top of the picture) with houses and shops on it and a chapel on the left
– the ships with their cargoes. Some in the front are covered vessels.
– the building between the White Tower and London Bridge, with the ships sailing up to it. This is the Customs' House where Chaucer once worked. It looks as if stores are being unloaded there.

What is happening inside the Tower of London? Who are riding out through the gateway?

There were gates in the walled city of London so that people could come in and go out. At one time Chaucer lived in rooms over the top of one of these gates, called Alde, or Old, Gate.

This picture shows two of the gates. We are inside the city walls, looking out over the countryside. Can you see the gate at the bottom in the middle of the picture? It is the Alde Gate. Pretend that you are standing on top of it and look around you. Notice:

—the countryside beyond the city wall

—the roads going in and out of the city. Along them came travellers from the north, on foot, on horseback or by carriage. Some of them hoped to make a fortune in London.

—the city wall. The wall is battlemented (like this ⌐⌐⌐⌐⌐) with turrets between the gates.

—churches with towers and, perhaps, a cross on top

—the fields and men in the fields. Can you guess what the men are doing? What are some of them holding? They are archers with bows and arrows, shooting at their targets. People liked archery then as much as we like football today.

—cows and goats. Do you think there are cows and goats just outside the city of London today? What is there instead?

Chaucer's view, looking from the Alde Gate, would have been of fields and trees like this—not at all like our present-day London.

If we climbed to the top of the Alde Gate and looked the other way, we would look towards the great River Thames. Here was the bustling city of London, with streets of houses built close together, and warehouses, wharves and boatyards.

Now look carefully at the picture above and find:
— the River Thames. How many different kinds of ships and boats are there?
— London Bridge with its houses and shops
— the Tower of London with a moat round it.

Between the Tower of London and London Bridge, at the water's edge, you will find the Customs' House, marked with an arrow. It is called Costume House. Can you remember who worked there as a Customs' officer?

To the right of the Customs' House, by the edge of the river, is a man with two beasts. What is he doing?

At the top right of the picture there is a woman. She has a basket and is spreading something on the ground to dry. Can you guess what it is?

8

There were lots of inns, or pubs, in 14th century London for people to amuse themselves in and many shops, but these looked just like ordinary houses. They had no windows for showing or displaying things for sale, because glass was very expensive. Inside the shops people could buy woollen cloth, silks and wooden or pottery bowls and plates. If they were rich they could buy silver and gold cups and jewels and things made of leather and fur. Food was not bought in shops, but in the street markets of London. There were also many churches for the large number of people who lived and worked in the town.

People lived over their shops and workrooms, or very near to the docks and markets. There were no trains or buses to bring workers into London from outside.

Towering over the city of London was St Paul's Cathedral on Ludgate Hill. St Paul's in Chaucer's day looked like this. There was a Bishop of London and this was his church. It had a tower *and* a spire and pointed windows.

Our present-day St Paul's is different as you can see here. It has a great dome. Try to find out why our St Paul's isn't at all like that of Chaucer's time and when and why our St Paul's was built. Remember that houses then were usually built of wood and that there were many fires in London.

Find out more about the Great Fire of London of 1666.

Pilgrims and pilgrimages

People leaving London for the south coast went over London Bridge and through Southwark on the road to Dover. From Dover they could sail to France. But many people went only as far as Canterbury, in Kent, to visit the cathedral and tomb, or shrine, of St Thomas Becket. St Thomas was the most popular English saint and Canterbury the most popular place of pilgrimage in England. Hundreds of pilgrims went there every year.

St Thomas, who had been born in the city of London, became Archbishop of Canterbury. In 1170 he was murdered by 4 knights in his cathedral, while trying to defend the rights of the Church. Some travellers, or pilgrims, said that miracles took place at St Thomas's shrine, so people went there hoping to be cured of their illnesses. Others went to see if people really were cured. Some went simply for the holiday and brought back little souvenirs, like those shown here, which were later found in excavations, or digs. Other pilgrims went to pray.

Pilgrimages are still made by many people in many parts of the world. Muslims go to Mecca, Christians to Jerusalem. Some English pilgrims went to Jerusalem in the 14th century, but it was a long and terrible journey across land and sea.

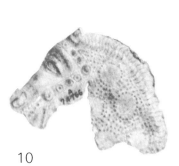

Where do you think these people are going? Describe how they are travelling. Notice:
— the bare feet of those who are walking
— the man on the right with his pilgrim's stick, called a scrip, which was used to clear the paths.

Some pilgrims were too poor to own or hire horses. Others did not even have shoes and some who had them did not wear them. They wanted to show St Thomas that they were humble people and that they did not mind suffering.

This pair of pilgrim's shoes is about 600 years old so they are very worn and torn. What do you think they are made of?

If you wanted to know what Britain looked like today, where London and Canterbury were, what roads they were on and how to get there, what would you do? You could go up in a helicopter, but you would see only one small area. It would be better to buy a map. There were maps of Britain in the 14th century. On the left is one of them. Find:

– London right down in the south on the River Thames (which looks like a branch of a tree)
– 'Cantuar', that is Canterbury (Canterbury is between London and 'Dova')
– 'Dova' on the south coast.

You can guess what town 'Dova' is if you say it aloud. Do you remember why people went to Dover?

The journey to Canterbury does not look very far, but the map is not drawn to scale. Also, the roads were narrow and muddy, which made travelling difficult. There were many potholes in them and when it rained these were filled with water. There was a story at the time that one traveller had fallen into a pothole which was so big that he drowned!

Southwark, on the road to Canterbury and Dover, became a busy and important place for travellers. The many inns in Southwark were filled with pilgrims leaving London for the south coast and others passing through Southwark on their way into London. Two such inns, where the weary travellers could rest, were 'The Tabard' and 'The George', which is shown here.

What is the inn built of? Why do you think it could catch fire easily?

The horses could come right up to the front of the inn. They were tied to the railings outside so that they could not gallop away. Inside the inn the travellers rested and refreshed themselves. Some met here and then travelled together in a party.

14th century men and women

During his travels Geoffrey Chaucer met all sorts of people and he wrote about some of them who were going from London to Canterbury on a pilgrimage. The book was called *The Canterbury Tales*. Chaucer was interested in everyone he met — how they dressed, talked, behaved and what jobs they had. In the following pages you can read about this group of pilgrims, from *The Canterbury Tales*, who set out one April morning from 'The Tabard Inn' in Southwark to ride to Canterbury.

The knight

First there was the knight. Knights had to fight for the king and command his troops. They were the officers in the king's army, of which the king was field marshal.

This picture shows a knight leaving for the wars (probably against the French) and saying goodbye to his wife and daughter. The knight is in armour. Notice:
— his helmet
— his spurs
— his lance, or spear
— his shield to stop other
    people's lances
    wounding him.

Chaucer's knight in *The Canterbury Tales* was rather old, as you can see in the picture. He no longer fought. He had retired from the wars. This is how Chaucer describes him:

'He was a very perfect, gentle knight.
But I shall tell you now of his array.
His horse was good, but still he was not gay.
He wore a doublet made of heavy wool,
Spotted with rust marks from his coat of mail;
For he was lately come from far away
And made his pilgrimage without delay.'

When knights were not fighting, they loved tournaments. Each knight rode on his horse and tried to unseat the other with his lance. Tournaments were great fun and knights were anxious to do well, especially as their ladies watched them.

The knights got ready in tents and then rode out to the sound of trumpets. They had the shutters, or visors, of their helmets closed, otherwise one or other might lose an eye. Their faces could not be seen so they had badges or symbols on top of their helmets so that people knew who they were.

In the picture the knight on the left has 4 feathers on his helmet. What does the knight on the right have as a badge? Who is winning? Find:

—the broken lance on the ground
—the ladies in their box
—another knight in the background who has horns on his helmet.

The squire or gentleman

This is the knight's son. He was called a 'squire', or gentleman. He is a very dashing young man on a lively, prancing horse and he wears fashionable clothes.

Read carefully each line of the poem below and look at the picture. Do you think the artist has drawn the squire as Chaucer described him?

Chaucer says:
'Of twenty years of age he was, I guess.
In stature he was of proper length
And wonderfully light and of great strength.

Embroidered was his tunic, like a mead [meadow]
Covered with springing flowers white and red.
Singing he was or fluting all the day.
He was as fresh as is the month of May.

Short was his gown, with sleeves both long and wide.
Well could he sit his horse and fairly ride.
Courteous he was, modest in mien [manner] and able,
And carved before his father at the table.'

16

Like Chaucer, the squire had learned to behave politely as a page in a nobleman's household. He had learned how to wait at table and how to carve, how to ride a horse well and how to fight in tournaments, or jousts.

The squire was a very fortunate young man. One day he would inherit his father's house and lands and live the comfortable life of a gentleman. He would marry and his wife would bring him more lands.

Here is a young squire out hunting with his friends. They would have hunted rabbits and foxes, as only the king was allowed to hunt deer. Dogs were used for hunting. How do we know from the picture that these gentlemen are hunting and not just going out for a ride?

Hawks, or falcons, were also used in hunting. Training the falcon to catch the prey, without hurting it, and then to return to the hunter's wrist, was a specialist's job. There were many books in the Middle Ages about how to do it and one of them was written by a 13th century emperor called Frederick II. People still train hawks today using the same methods.

Many English kings (like William Rufus who was killed by an arrow while hunting in the New Forest) loved hunting.

The franklin or wealthy freeman

In the 14th century not all men were free to do what they liked and few men owned their land and house or cottage. In fact, most men had to do certain tiresome jobs, or services, for their landlords. For example, they had to sow and cut his corn and look after his animals.

Later on in this book you can read more about these men, the peasants, and how they rose up and objected to their treatment.

So the freeman, or franklin, who owned his own house and some land, was quite an important man and some franklins were very rich. Chaucer's franklin had been a Member of Parliament, or as it was then called 'Knight of the Shire', at Westminster. The picture on the left shows a franklin called Walter de Helyon, who came from Much Marcle in Herefordshire. It is from his tomb and shows him as a young man. He is wearing indoor clothing.

The picture below shows Chaucer's franklin well wrapped up in his outdoor clothing. Notice the franklin's belt in both pictures and what is hanging from it – a dagger to protect him and a purse for his money.

Chaucer describes his franklin like this:

'His cupboard was never without a pie
Of fish or flesh, and such a good supply
His house contained, it snowed of meat and drink
And all the dainties that a man can think.

Many a partridge fat he had in mew [in a cage]
And many a bream and many a pike in stew.
Full oft he had been chosen Knight of Shire.
A dagger and a wallet all of silk
Hung at his girdle, white as morning milk.'

Do you remember what a Knight of Shire was?

This is the front and back of a purse
which was found in the ditch outside
the walls of the city of London, where
people threw their rubbish and
unwanted objects. The purse does not
look worn enough to be thrown away.

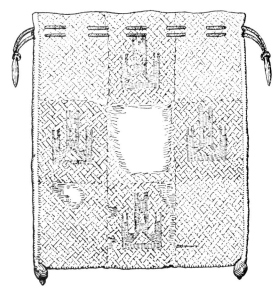

Make a purse like this with some
material and cord and paint castles,
swans, fleurs-de-lys or stars on it, as if
it is your badge.

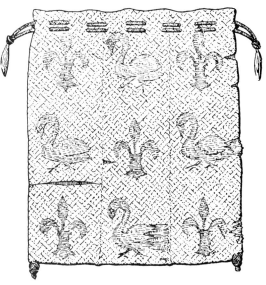

If your name is Franklin, you will know
now that your ancestors were freemen.
Or perhaps your name is Smith — smiths
were blacksmiths who shoed horses
and mended carts. Or perhaps your
name is Carpenter — what did your
ancestors do? Try to think of other
names which come from people's work.
    Did you think of Draper, Butcher,
Mercer, Wheeler, Clark? A mercer was
a draper. A wheeler made wheels. Clark,
or Clerk, means someone who was a
clergyman or scholar.

The clerk

In the 14th century there were two universities, or places of learning, in England — Oxford and Cambridge. In the picture you can see the clerks, or scholars, in an Oxford college. Can you pick out the master and the teachers? They are wearing black caps. The students look quiet and are paying attention. In the background you can see:
- the clerks' rooms with the tall chimney pots
- the tower of the chapel
- the dining hall with steps leading up to it
- the gateway into the college.

Each college had rooms for the students and the masters, a dining hall, a chapel and a library. They were all built round a square, called a quadrangle, or 'quad' for short.

If you go to Oxford and visit New College you will find that it hasn't changed much since this picture was drawn. The college was built by William of Wykeham the wealthy Bishop of Winchester in 1379, so it was 'New' College in Chaucer's day.

Here is Chaucer's clerk. You will know why he carries a book. Chaucer says that he was 'not too fat, but looked hollow', and that 'the thread upon his overcoat was bare'. His horse was 'leaner than a rake'. Why do you think his horse looks thin? Can you see its ribs?

The clerk spent all his money on books, pens and ink. Here are two ink wells like those the clerks would have used.

The clerk had little hope of making a fortune, at least not until he had passed his exams. Most people in 14th century England could not read or write so those who could were needed by the king for his civil service. These were the clerks who carried out the government work for the king, writing and issuing his orders.

The merchant

There were many merchants in
London and in the ports of Bristol
and Southampton. They traded in
certain goods – furs, wine and,
above all, wool and woollen cloth.
Chaucer's merchant traded from
Harwich in Essex to Holland.
Another merchant sent
goods from Ipswich in
Suffolk to Middelburgh in
the Low Countries. We
now call the Low
Countries Holland and
Belgium. Find Holland
and Belgium in an atlas.

Chaucer describes his
merchant as having:
– a forked beard
– daintily buckled boots
– a high fur hat.
   Can you find these things in the picture? What else is he wearing?

The wool which the merchants exported came from flocks of sheep in Yorkshire,
the Cotswolds and East Anglia. Great stretches of England were used to rear sheep
– fells, dales and moors – and later on people complained that the sheep were
pushing men out of their villages. They said that there were so many sheep that the
sheep were taking over.

In the autumn the sheep were sheared and the wool was put into bales and sent
to London and then sold to people in Europe. There the wool was woven into cloth
and clothes – coats, stockings, cloaks. But some of the cloth was woven in England
and English cloths were world famous. Many merchants exported these cloths to
distant places and became rich.

Here are merchants
at the quayside.
What is being
unloaded? Notice:
– the winch, or
   crane, with the
   chains which are
   lifting up the
   barrels
– the person inside
   the crane and the
   man unloading the
   barrels off the
   chains.

How many ships
with masts and sails
can you see? Some
of the sails are
rolled up.
   What do you think
the merchants are
saying to one
another? They might
be talking about the
tides or the winds
and weather. Or
perhaps they are
talking about the
money they have
made and what they
have to pay to the
Customs' officer.

Some of the merchants wrote letters home while they
were abroad, telling of their business deals and travels
and seeking news of their families. From these letters
we know much about what a merchant's life was like.

England became very rich from her sheep and wool; not only the merchants and the sheep-farmers, but also the king who put taxes on wool.

In our parliament today the Lord Chancellor sits on a wool-sack, or bale of wool, to show how England became rich. Look at this picture of the House of Lords and pick out the wool-sack with the cushion on it.

One merchant built a big house with the money he made from selling wool. When it was finished, he had written on one of the windows:

'I praise God, and ever shall,
It is the sheep who have paid for all.'

Some of our parish churches have fine 'brasses', or monuments, of wool merchants. At Chipping Camden church there is the brass of William Grevil, 'late citizen of London and flower of the wool merchants of all England' and his wife. He died in 1401 but you can still see his house in the village street. Find out whether there are any wool towns and brasses near to where you live.

25

The sea captain

You will remember that cloth and wool were exported abroad and that wine and other goods were brought into our ports, so there were plenty of jobs on ships. Here is Chaucer's sea captain, or skipper, from Dartmouth in Devon. He knew all about 'moons, harbours and pilots' and where to shelter in storms. His ship was called *The Magdalen*.

These fashionable ladies and gentlemen are landing at Boulogne in France. They had set sail from Dover. Their clothes and goods are in the trunks. Notice:

– the lady's maid with the hand luggage
– the porter carrying the trunk on his back
– the sailor rolling up the sail because the ship is in port.

Did you notice the crow's-nest at the top of the ship's mast? What was this used for?

The doctor

The doctor in the picture is carrying a bottle. He seems to be taking care not to spill the contents. It was best not to fall ill in 14th century England because there were some nasty cures. The royal doctor, John of Gaddesden, made his patients swallow black beetles and fat bats! No wonder people preferred to go on pilgrimages in the hope of being cured! Many said: 'For good people who are sick, St Thomas Becket is the best of physicians.'

But John of Gaddesden was a clever man. He had studied at Oxford. He knew how to cure smallpox. He wrapped the patient in a red blanket and doctors have since discovered that red light actually does heal smallpox scars.

Only the rich could afford to pay doctors. In this picture a rich patient is lying in bed, while the doctor consults with his colleagues about the treatment. The patient doesn't look very happy. Perhaps he fears a dose of beetles! Look carefully at the picture and find:
– the doctor and his colleagues
– the pillow and bolster
– the ornate hangings over the bed. These hangings were to keep the draughts out, especially in winter.

Poor people, especially in the country, tried cures from herbs and herbalists, or sellers of herbs and other medicines, who went round the fairs and inns. For most people who became ill there were no cures if the herbalist's bottles failed.

The woman from Bath

Among the pilgrims who went to Canterbury with Geoffrey Chaucer, was a woman from the town of Bath in Somerset. She had had 5 husbands. She loved travelling and going on pilgrimages. She had been 3 times to Jerusalem and also to Rome and to Cologne in Germany. Mountain passes and muddy roads, hard beds and foreign food didn't put her off travelling. She liked, says Chancer, 'to laugh and chat' and wore on her head an enormous hat.

Look at her hat which is tied over her wimple, or headscarf. She is carrying a crop in her hand because she liked to ride at a spanking pace. Chaucer says:

> 'Her stockings were a scarlet red
> And tightly tied; her shoes were soft and new.
> Bold was her face and fair and red of hue.'

In Bath she was known as a first-rate weaver of cloth. This is the kind of loom she would have used. Find the needle, or shuttle, taking the threads across. All cloth was woven by hand in this way.

The lawyer

People need lawyers when they buy property or when they get into trouble. Lawyers know how to draft, or compose, deeds and they know all the laws that have been made. The main courts of law, where very important cases were heard by the judges, were in London and are still there today. There were also courts held in the counties.

If you wished to become a lawyer it was necessary to go to London to study at one of the 'inns of court'. The inns of court were like the Oxford colleges, but in them you could only study law — not medicine, theology, mathematics or science, as at Oxford or Cambridge.

The picture above is of the hall of Lincoln's Inn, where the law students studied.

Chaucer's lawyer, whom you see here, had risen to the high position of a judge. He had tried many cases, knew all the laws and penalties and had made much money from practising the law.

The miller

Corn had to be ground to make flour for bread. This was done by hand, but it was hard work. Usually the lord of the manor, or owner of the land, had a windmill or a water-mill for grinding corn. The wind turned the sails, or the water turned the wheel, and the grain became fine flour. The lord made all the men in the village use his mill, but not free of charge. He took a sack of flour from each man. Sometimes the miller, too, secretly kept a bag for himself.

Study this picture carefully. Notice:
- the miller taking a bag of corn for grinding
- the man on horseback, sitting on a bag of corn which he is taking to the mill
- the whip the man is using to urge his horse on (like the woman from Bath on page 28)
- the steps up to the mill which were to stop rats and mice coming in and eating the corn
- the dog. Can you guess why the miller kept a dog?

The mill itself is on a post. What is the special name for this type of mill?

Chaucer's miller, Robin, whom you can see in the picture, was a big, fat fellow and weighed 100 kg. He was very strong. He could wrestle and take any door off its hinges. He had a red face and a large mouth. He wore a huge sword and played a musical instrument to the pilgrims as they journeyed along. If you look carefully at the picture, you will see what kind of musical instrument he is playing.

The cook

There were plenty of cooks in 14th century England — cooks in great houses, cooks in inns and cooks who owned cooked-meat shops.

This room is the kitchen in a medieval house. Find:
— the grate and fire, where the meat would have been roasted on spits
— the kitchen cupboard for stores
— the trough, on the right, for salting meat
— the hugh block, on the left, for chopping. Perhaps there is a working top in your kitchen, but not quite so big!

Important people did not do the cooking themselves but employed cooks to do it for them. The cook in a great household was a very important person, like the chef in a large hotel or restaurant. He had many assistants to pound the spices, turn the spits and carry the great pans to and fro.

When the meat was taken to be roasted, or to be salted, a tool was used called a flesh-hook, like the one you see here.

Chaucer's pilgrims had hired their cook from a London cook-shop to travel with them and to prepare and cook their food on the journey. Look at this picture of the cook. How do we know that he *is* the cook? Did you notice his apron and his flesh-hook? This cook could make a good thick soup and bake a tasty pie, but nothing was so delicious as his blancmange.

Most people in 14th century England did not eat as well as this. Their food was bread, beans and ale; sometimes a little cheese or eggs, perhaps. Ordinary people could not afford much meat and many did not get enough to eat. They were lucky if they ever tasted a nice pie and they wouldn't have known what a blancmange was.

There were frequent food shortages, particularly, of course, if there was not enough rain and the harvests were bad. Little was known about storing food and nothing was known about vitamins.

There were no refrigerators in the 14th century, so salt was used to preserve the meat. Cupboards, like this one, had air holes, or vents, in them to keep the food cool.

The reeve

Last of all the pilgrims came this man, Oswald the reeve, on his horse called Scot. The reeve was the lord's steward, or officer, in the village. He was like a foreman who saw that the peasants did their work properly for the lord, so he was not very popular in the village. The workers felt that he spied on them, reporting them to the lord if they did not work. He stood over them, too, when they were working and told them when to take a rest.

Below is the reeve, with his horn, supervising the peasants.

Chaucer's reeve, Oswald, had a nice house on a heath near his village in Norfolk. The villagers envied him, but they also feared him, as Chaucer says 'like the plague'.

The reeve, however, knew all about how to get good crops and how to look after the animals well for his master, the lord. Every September, or Michaelmas, he had to draw up the accounts of everything spent in the village and of all the money which the lord received from the crops and animals. He had to make the books 'balance' and the lord was not very pleased if there were no profits.

Make yourselves into small groups of peasants. Your teacher can choose a lord and a reeve. Now mime a scene between peasants, reeve and lord. You can find out more about life on the land on pages 41 to 43.

14th century church people

Many people worked for the Church in medieval England. There were parsons, archdeacons and bishops, who looked after people in the towns and in the countryside. There were also religious people who lived in convents. There were convents (or monasteries) for men, who were called monks, and convents (or nunneries) for women, who were called nuns.

The parson

Everybody knew the parson, or parish priest, because he baptised the children, married people and buried them when they died. He looked after them and advised them. Most people could not read or write, but the parson could, so he did that for them, too. In the church he told them about God and said they should be kind to one another and get on with their work.

The parson also told his superior, the archdeacon, when the people didn't behave and when they didn't pay their taxes to the Church. The archdeacon could punish them by fining them or by throwing them into gaol. If the archdeacon was not sure whether they had behaved badly or not, he could bring them to court. The archdeacon's court then decided what should happen to them.

Not all parsons in 14th century England were good, but Chaucer's parson was:

'Though wide his parish, houses far asunder,
He held not back even in rain and thunder
From seeking those in sickness or distress,
Whether nearby or in the farthest place.

To draw folk into heaven by holiness
And good example was his business.
The word of Christ and His Apostles twelve
He taught, but first he followed it himself.'

This picture shows the village church at Lacock in Wiltshire. Notice:
- the spire and weather cock
- the ornate windows.

The summoner

The archdeacon had a 'summoner' to summon, or order, people to court. The summoner was usually a bully of a man. He was not a clergyman, so he didn't wear the habit, or frock, of the monk and parson. Instead he wore coloured stockings and an anorak, or doublet.

Look at this picture of Chaucer's summoner. What has he in his right hand? (Did you guess that it is a letter ordering someone to court?) Where is his sword-case, or sheath, and his purse?

Make a colourful picture of the summoner riding into a village and up to a cottage to summon someone to the archdeacon's court. This description of him may help you:

> 'A summoner was with us in that place
> Who had a fiery red, cherubic face.
> With scarred black brows and very little beard
> His face was something all the children feared.'

The monk

In the Middle Ages many young men went into convents, or monasteries, and became monks. The monastery was like a large school or college and the monk lived there. Monks took 3 vows, or made 3 promises: not to marry, to obey the abbot, or head of the monastery, and to give up all their personal possessions.

Monks were supposed to follow a set of rules which their founder, St Benedict, had made for them. The rules said that they were to eat simple food, like bread, porridge and vegetables, and to dress in plain and cheap clothes. Each day they spent some hours in church praying, some in reading or studying and some in seeing to the business of the convent. They were not allowed to go out of the monastery when they felt like it and, of course, they were not supposed to go hunting, or 'to the chase' as it was called. But there were always some monks who did not keep all the rules and some abbots who were not very strict.

Read carefully Chaucer's description of the monk and look at the picture.

'A Monk there was, full worthy of his place
An outrider who doted on [loved] the chase.
Why should he study? Why should he go mad
In some dark cell, poring upon a book?

Why labour with his hands, or sweat, or work?
Greyhounds he had as swift as birds in flight.
In tracking and in hunting of the hare
Was all his joy, and no cost would he spare.

His sleeves were ornamented at the hand
With soft grey fur, the finest in the land.
He was not pale as a lamented ghost.
A fat swan loved he best of any roast.'

Find his hunting dogs, or greyhounds, in the picture.
Did the rules of St Benedict allow this?
What does Chaucer say about the sleeves of his clothes? Was he breaking the rules in dressing like this? What was his favourite dish?

You can read more about monks in *Life in the Medieval Monastery* in the *Focus on History* series.

The friar

There were always some monks who thought that the rules were not strict enough or that they were not being properly kept. These men might go off and found a new monastery. There were some monks, called Cistercians, who tried to follow St Benedict's rules exactly and they built their monasteries in remote places away from people.

About 100 years before Chaucer was born, two holy men, St Francis and St Dominic, thought that the people in the towns needed to be told about the teachings of Christ and that the monks were not doing this. So the two men built their friaries in the towns, preached to the people and advised them. At first the friars were much admired because they lived simply like the poor people themselves.

Below is the Greyfriars' (or followers of St Francis) house at Canterbury. It was much like a monastery but not so big and grand.

By Chaucer's time some of the friars, like the monks, were rather lazy and greedy. Chaucer says that his friar, whom you see above and who was called Hubert, was good at begging, went often to taverns, or inns, and could play the hurdy-gurdy, or barrel-organ. Does he sound like a good and dutiful friar?

37

The prioress

Some of the girls became nuns and went to live in convents called nunneries. The head of the nunnery was called the prioress. Nuns took the same 3 vows as monks. Many nuns lived like ordinary ladies in their nunneries, though they were not allowed to marry. They had lap dogs and they ate sweets. Sometimes widowed ladies retired to live in convents and many rich people sent their daughters to convents to be educated, because nuns ran boarding schools. Three of the most important nunneries in England were at Wilton, Amesbury and Cambridge.

The picture above shows Chaucer's prioress. Her name was Madam Eglantine. She was very ladylike. She spoke nicely and had good manners. She ate daintily and quietly, without dropping her food. She is riding side-saddle as ladies did then. Find:
— her hood with a wimple, or white scarf, under it. She is showing her forehead, which a nun was not supposed to do.
— her bracelet. Nuns were not allowed to wear jewellery.
— the ornamented harness on her horse.

Here is the prioress's chaplain. She took him with her on her journey to Canterbury to say the services for her, because according to the rules of the Church she was not allowed to say them herself.

The pardoner

In the 14th century, if you had done something wrong, you might buy a pardon from the pope, who was the head of the whole Church. The pardons were sold by men called 'pardoners'. But some pardons did not come from the pope at all. The pardoners wrote the letters themselves (saying that the pope forgave so-and-so for some wicked action) and went round selling them. Before they sold the pardons, they reminded the people of all their wicked deeds and told them that when they died they would fall into the fires of hell if they didn't buy a pardon.

The pope, of course, did not approve of this. He only pardoned people when they were really sorry, but he could not stop the pardoners and their stories.

Look at the picture of a pardoner and notice:
— the cross he carries to remind people of their sins
— the big bag, or satchel, round the horse's neck. What do you think is inside it?
— his hat. The badge on it is of one of the saints. It reminded people that they could buy little relics, or souvenirs of saints, from him.

Here is a bigger picture of a bag, similar to the pardoner's bag, for you to look at.

Travelling through the countryside

Half-way along 'the Pilgrims' Way' between London and Canterbury, the pilgrims came to Rochester. What river is Rochester on? What was the road called which the pilgrims followed? It was a very old road, which the Romans had built.

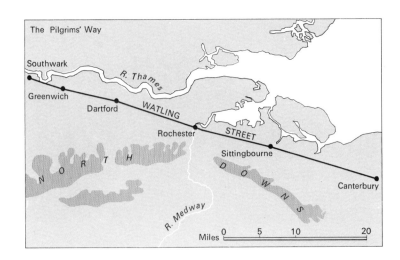

Using the scale on the map, work out how far the pilgrims had come. They had passed through the small villages of Greenwich and Dartford. It was countryside the whole way.

As the pilgrims crossed Rochester Bridge, the view below is what they saw.
Find:
—the castle with its fine Norman keep, or central tower
—the cathedral.

To pass the time as they rode along, the pilgrims told stories to one another— stories of what they had seen and heard, stories of towns and villages; stories, in fact, of what life was like in the 14th century.

Most people worked on the land in 14th century England. The work was never finished and went on in the same way from year to year.

In the autumn they ploughed. As you can see from the picture, they did not use horses to pull the plough. What animals did they use? How are the oxen fastened to the plough? Nowadays farmers use tractors instead, but the plough itself is much the same. Find the coulter, or iron blade, which cut the earth and made a channel, or furrow, for the seeds to be sown in rows. What are the two men doing? What clothes are they wearing?

After ploughing, the farmer sowed the crop. He brought the seeds on to the fields in a sack and placed some of them in a wooden basket, which he hung round his neck. He then walked up and down between the furrows, throwing the seed from either hand as he walked.

Look at the picture and find:
— the sack of seed
— the wooden basket, called a hopper.
Who liked to eat the seed? How did the farmer stop them?

This picture shows another way to scare off crows. Look carefully and you will see what it is. (Perhaps you have seen a 'scarecrow' used for the same purpose.) These men are harrowing, or covering the seed with soil, so that it will grow. The harrow was a wooden frame. It had teeth under it to cover the seed as the harrow was drawn along. What animal is pulling the harrow?

When the corn had grown it had to be cut or harvested. The farm worker, or peasant, had to cut his lord's corn, too, so he was very busy. Everyone—men, women and children—had to help with the harvesting.

What are the women doing in this picture? What is the curved knife called which they are using? Harvesting was a back-breaking task and so the harvesters look tired and weary.

When the corn had been cut it had to be tied into bundles, or sheaves, and stacked up to dry in a rick.

What are the people doing in the picture above? Find those who are wearing gloves — one man has them in his belt. Stacking sheaves without gloves made the hands very sore.

Finally the peasants loaded the sheaves on to the cart so that they could be taken to the lord's barn. Describe what each person is doing in this picture. The horses look lively, but the load is very heavy.

When the peasant had finished harvesting, he didn't have a holiday. Instead he had to start ploughing again for the next year!

Great happenings and great people of the times

The Black Death

When Chaucer was a boy, a great plague swept across England. It was known as the Black Death. This picture shows people carrying the coffins of those who had died to the hastily-dug graves.

Possibly one half of the population of England died as a result of the Black Death. We do not know the exact number. But we know that there were churches without parsons and villages like ghost towns. Things would not be the same again. Someone died in every family and sometimes whole families died. A chronicler, or reporter of the times, wrote:

> 'In this year 1348, in Melcombe, in the county of Dorset, two ships, one of them from Bristol, came alongside. One of the sailors had brought with him from Gascony the terrible pestilence and, through him, the men of that town of Melcombe were the first in England to be infected.'

Look at these crosses. They were made during the plague year in memory of those who died from the Black Death. As you can see, they were made in a hurry and were buried along with the victims in a common grave in the Greyfriars' cemetery in the city of London.

When the parson had died and there was no one to bury the people, the corpses were hurriedly thrown into common graves to prevent other people catching the plague.

The Peasants' Revolt

People were very unsettled after the Black Death and especially unhappy about working for their lords. They had to work even harder because there were now fewer workers to do all the jobs on the land. They disliked the way in which their services for their lords were all written down and the way in which they were supervised, or bossed, by the reeve.

When the peasants' revolt began, the workers burned the records so that nobody would know exactly what services they had to perform for their lords. The peasants felt particularly angry with the lords and churchmen who owned a great deal of land and who did nothing to improve the peasants' working conditions. At St Albans the peasants rushed into the abbey and ransacked and looted the place.

The leaders of those who wanted to change things were John Ball and Wat Tyler. They organised this first workers' revolution, or 'peasants' revolt'. John Ball was a parson. He did not think it right that some men should be rich and some poor. He said:

'When Adam dug and Eve span [spun]
Who was then the gentleman?'

This picture shows John Ball gathering together his followers. Many of them are wearing crosses on their coats. What else are they wearing and what weapons are they carrying? John Ball is preaching to them from his horse. He is telling them to rise up and follow him.

Wat Tyler was a discontented soldier. He and John Ball gathered together a vast crowd of supporters. On 11th June 1381, they began their march on London. At Blackheath they asked to speak to King Richard II. When this was prevented, they marched on to London and freed the prisoners from the gaols. When they arrived at Lambeth Palace, they seized the archbishop of Canterbury, Simon Sudbury, dragged him to Tower Hill and murdered him.

The rebels wanted 3 things:
1. no lords except the king 2. all men to be equal 3. the riches of the Church to be taken and shared among the poor. But the rebels were put down thanks to the bravery of the young king, Richard, who rode out, almost alone, to meet them at Smithfield. They did not get what they wanted. Wat Tyler was killed by the Mayor of London and the revolt was at an end.

This picture shows two scenes. First, on the right, the king is speaking to the rebels and advising them to go home. Secondly, on the left, the Mayor of London, who was called William Walworth, is about to behead Wat Tyler.

Describe what happened, as if you were one of the men at Smithfield in 1381.

The two popes

At this time in Europe there were two popes and men did not know which one to obey. One pope was in Rome and the other was in Avignon, in the south of France. The English favoured and supported the pope who lived in Rome, but no one could be sure who was the rightful, or real, pope.

Here is the French pope's palace at Avignon. Find the pope's church, the castle, the walls of the city and the river.

With two popes, it was not surprising that no one knew whether the pardoners' letters were true or false. Everyone was confused. Even the archbishops and bishops did not know what to do.

This picture shows the archbishop of Canterbury reading a letter from the pope to his congregation.
Notice:
– the archbishop's mitre, or hat
– the pope's letter with the seal attached.

Here is a mitre, with its box for carrying it about.
Archbishops, bishops and kings were always travelling and the pilgrims may have passed the archbishop or the king on their way to Canterbury.

47

The wars with France

The pilgrims might also have passed soldiers on their way to Dover and so to France. One of the reasons why the English supported the pope in Rome was because the French supported the pope in Avignon. The English and French did not get on at all well. The English were overlords of almost one-third of France in 1360. But this was not to last and there were revolts against English rule. The wars were later called the 'Hundred Years' War' because they went on for so long.

In 1369 the English lost the county of Ponthieu, in 1373 Poitou and in 1374 Aquitaine. After that there were English garrisons at only Calais, Brest and Bordeaux, from which the English attacked the French now and again.

King Richard II tried to end the wars with the French because they were so costly and in 1396 he married the French princess, Isabella. So until Richard died in 1399 there were a few years of peace between England and France.

Find on the map:
— the main English possessions — Ponthieu, Poitou, Aquitaine and Gascony
— the towns of Calais, Brest and Bordeaux, where the English garrisons were.

Write a diary of the military campaigns from 1360 to 1374, as if you were a soldier in the English (or French) army.

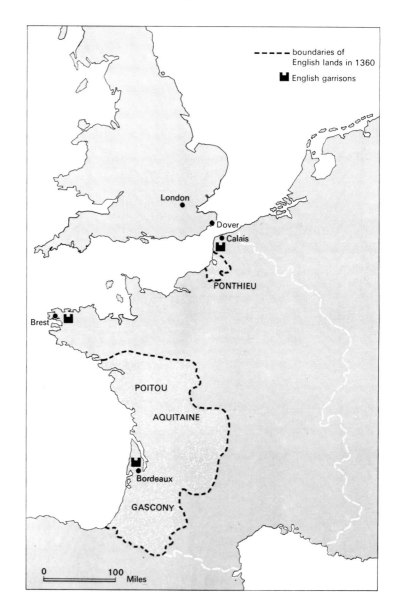

48

King Richard II and his uncles

When Chaucer was born, King Edward III ruled England. Edward III had 7 sons, including Edward the Black Prince; Lionel, Duke of Clarence; John of Gaunt, Duke of Lancaster; Edmund, Duke of York; and Thomas, Duke of Gloucester. This diagram shows part of the family tree.

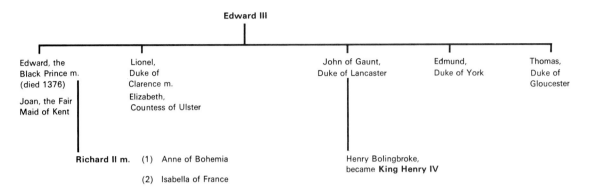

Edward III

Edward, the Black Prince m. (died 1376) — Joan, the Fair Maid of Kent

Lionel, Duke of Clarence m. — Elizabeth, Countess of Ulster

John of Gaunt, Duke of Lancaster

Edmund, Duke of York

Thomas, Duke of Gloucester

Richard II m.   (1)   Anne of Bohemia
          (2)   Isabella of France

Henry Bolingbroke, became **King Henry IV**

As you can see from the family tree, Richard II was the son of Edward, the Black Prince. Now look carefully at the family tree and decide:
—what relation Richard II was to John of Gaunt
—what relation Richard II was to Henry Bolingbroke.

Edward III died in 1377 after a reign of 50 years. His grandson, Richard II, succeeded him. Can you guess why Edward the Black Prince did not succeed his father as King of England?

Look at this marvellous sculpture of Edward III as an old man. You can see it among the royal tombs in Westminster Abbey. Notice the wrinkles on his forehead, the long beard and the wavy hair.

Make a family tree of your own family.

Edward the Black Prince was a brave and gallant knight who wore black armour and so was nicknamed 'the Black Prince'. He had fought at the battles of Crécy in 1346 and Poitiers in 1355, where the English won great victories, and had taken the French king prisoner. Edward died in 1376.

This photograph of his tomb in Canterbury Cathedral shows you the armour of a knight. Find:
- the helmet
- the gauntlets, or gloves
- the chain-mail round his head
- the diadem, or small crown, on his head.

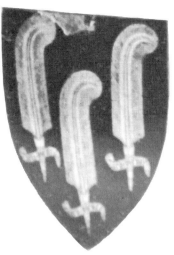

All round the tomb are shields. Here are two of them. The design of the leopards and lilies is also in the picture above.

As the king's eldest son, the Black Prince was Prince of Wales and so had the badge of the Prince of Wales – 3 feathers, with the motto 'I serve'.

The most powerful of King Edward III's sons and of King Richard II's uncles was John of Gaunt, Duke of Lancaster. He was born in 1340 and died in 1399. He had a son called Henry Bolingbroke.

John of Gaunt had plenty of money and power. He entertained visitors grandly. Here he is playing host to the King of Portugal, who is seated in the middle, holding a royal rod, or sceptre, and wearing an ermine cape. Can you find John of Gaunt, who is also wearing an ermine cape?

Look again at the picture and then answer the following questions:
—who are the other guests?
—where are the serving people?
—what are the visitors going to eat?
—where are the musicians?
—what can you see on the table?

Here is the hall of John of Gaunt's palace at Kenilworth, where he entertained the King of Portugal, as it is now. Where do you think the serving hatch was and the high table?

51

Richard II was only 10 years old when his grandfather died in 1377 and he became king. He was crowned at Westminster. As he was so young, his uncles ruled the kingdom in his name. The wars with France went badly. Richard wanted to rule his kingdom himself and to make peace with the French, but he was not given good advice by his counsellors.

Richard was very interested in books and pictures, and in writers and artists. He encouraged men to write books and paint pictures. His court was a fashionable place. Men wore long pointed shoes, curious hats and short capes with padded shoulders. You can see all these things in the picture.

You can also see a writer, called John Froissart, presenting the king with his book. Much of what we know about life in England in the 14th century has come from reading Froissart's book.

Richard's reign ended sadly. He was badly advised and unsuccessful in war and so was unable to please the great nobles. He quarrelled with his cousin, Henry Bolingbroke, and exiled or sent him from the kingdom. Then he began to rule more and more on his own, without asking advice from his nobles. From then onwards Henry Bolingbroke was Richard's enemy and in 1399 he returned to England with an army. He marched to Conway Castle and made Richard surrender to him and give up the throne, or abdicate. Henry not only claimed the throne for himself because of Richard's misrule, but also because he had a claim to it by birth. The picture below shows Richard II and his men at Conway Castle.

Richard was then imprisoned at Pontefract Castle and when his men rose up against Henry Bolingbroke, Henry ordered Richard to be murdered. Henry took the crown for himself as King Henry IV.

Henry was a very different character from Richard. He was more interested in sport and fighting than in pictures and books. As the son of John of Gaunt, he inherited all the land which his father had owned as Duke of Lancaster, and had the support of the important earls (the Lords Percy and Neville) in the north of England.

William Shakespeare later wrote a play about the tragic, or sad, life of King Richard II and also one about Henry IV.

This double picture is one of the most precious in the National Gallery in London. The young king, Richard II, is kneeling in prayer to the baby Christ and his mother.

Richard's followers wore the badge of the white hart, or deer. If you look carefully you will see that the king's cloak, or mantle, is covered with white harts and that he is wearing a white hart on a chain round his neck. Who else are wearing the badge of the white hart?

Canterbury—the end of the journey

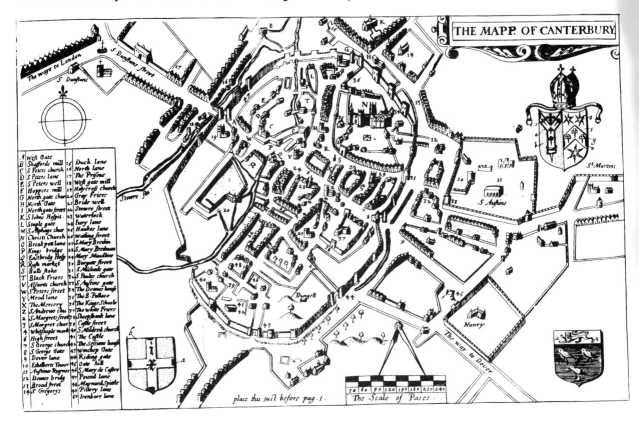

THE MAPP. OF CANTERBURY

place this just before pag. 1.

The Scale of Paces.

After several days riding, Chaucer's pilgrims approached the city of Canterbury. (The map shows the road to and from London at the top left.) Then they rode down St Dunstans Street to their lodgings and the cathedral.

Look carefully at the map and find:
— the walls of the city
— the gates in and out of the city
— the main street, or high street, running from the West Gate to St George's Gate at the east end.

One or two of the hostelries, or inns, were outside the city walls, others were in Mercery Lane (marked X) and in Burgate Street (marked 30). Find the cathedral (marked N) where the shrine of St Thomas was.

Canterbury looked much like any other medieval city with its walls and gates. See if you can find out what any of the following cities were like at that time:

Bristol	Exeter	Norwich	Southampton
Chester	King's Lynn	Oxford	Winchester
Durham	Lancaster	Shrewsbury	York

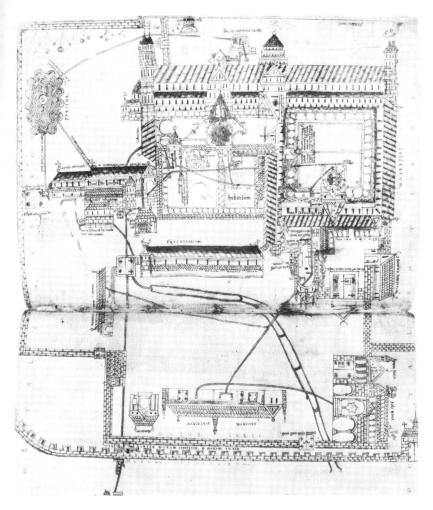

The cathedral at Canterbury was also a monastery which housed about 80 monks. It was like a city within a city. This map shows what it looked like when there were monks there. The monks had their own refectory, or canteen, dormitory, kitchen, bakehouse, brewhouse and garden. The monks also had their own water supply and a hospital for those who were sick.

Look at the map and find:
— the church (at the top) with its towers and turrets
— the walls round the monastery (at the bottom and on the left)
— the gates (bottom right) into the monastery.

Monks were not supposed to go frequently out of the monastery, as you will remember, and never without the permission of the abbot. Many of the townspeople depended on the monastery for their jobs. They worked as cleaners, cooks and domestic servants.

If you look again at page 56 you will see the great church of the monastery within its own walls and with its own gates. Did you notice that one wall is formed by a row of houses and shops belonging to the townspeople? There was a street market just outside the main gate of the monastery where butter, bulls and rushes were sold.

There was another monastery in Canterbury, as well as the cathedral, where monks followed the rule of St Benedict. It was called St Augustine's, or St Austin's. There was also a nunnery for women. You can find them both if you look to the right of the plan on page 56.

This great gateway (which looks like a castle) was the pilgrims' entrance into the city of Canterbury. Over the bridge on the left they went, crossing the River Stour, through the West Gate and past the church of the Holy Cross (on the right).

There were several mills on the River Stour. Perhaps you have a Mill Street in your town. If so, there must have been a mill there at some time for grinding flour.

Canterbury also had several hospitals, where the old and sick were looked after, a prison for wrong-doers, a castle to defend the city, two friaries and, of course, many houses and churches.

Traders lived in separate quarters, or areas, in medieval towns — the butchers in one quarter, the mercers, or drapers, in another and the bakers in yet another. In Canterbury there is a Butchery Lane, a Mercery Lane and a Bakers' Lane.

All the Jews, too, lived in one part of the town, because they spoke the same language, Hebrew, and had the same customs.

58

Mercery Lane in Canterbury, where the drapers had their shops, is still the same width today as it was in the 14th century. The houses and shops were so close that people could almost shake hands across the street.

Pilgrims stayed at the inn, on the left, called 'The Chequers of Hope'. It had a great room upstairs called the 'dormitory of the hundred beds'. The pilgrims were very close to the cathedral. You can see the gate into the cathedral at the end of the lane. There was a lot to do and a lot to see, but to see the shrine of St Thomas in the cathedral was the pilgrims' main aim.

Here is the inside of a mercer's shop. Shops did not have glass windows as they do now. People had to step inside to see the goods—in this case, combs, mirrors and ribbons.

Before they left, most people bought souvenirs, like these, from the shops to show that they had been to Canterbury. The souvenirs were badges, which they hung on themselves or their horses or took back home as presents. They were usually pictures of St Thomas, sometimes of him on horseback, sometimes of his head and sometimes of his murder by the knights. You could also buy little 'Canterbury' bells, which were made of silver.

There were no postcards in the 14th century, so news of your journey had to wait until you got home. No doubt some travellers kept diaries so that they remembered every exciting detail to tell their friends and neighbours. There were no cameras either, so they had to describe it all themselves.

The great nave of Canterbury cathedral, which you can see here, was built at just about the time when Chaucer's pilgrims came to Canterbury.

The pilgrims would have gone along the nave, up the stairs to the choir, through the door at the end and then up the much-worn 'pilgrims' steps' to the holy of holies — Becket's Crown. There they found the shrine, or tomb, of the saint. They were not allowed to get too near the shrine nor to stay too long.

Monks guarded the shrine, raised the canopy over it, saw that the pilgrims were orderly and well-behaved and collected the gifts of money which the pilgrims made to the saint.

This stained glass in the cathedral was made in the 13th century and shows us what the shrine looked like. It was long and low with two oval openings. Below are some pilgrims approaching it, while the monks stand by.

Thousands of people flocked to Canterbury every year. The shops and inns of the city flourished because of all the pilgrims who came and stayed and bought things. In 1420 as many as 100,000 pilgrims visited Canterbury. (Do you remember how many people lived in the city of London? If not, look back to page 6.)

Here is a picture of the saint-archbishop, Thomas Becket, whom they all came to see. There must have been no richer sight than the tomb of St Thomas, covered with sparkling, flashing and glowing jewels, including an enormous ruby which had been given by King Louis VII of France.

One story was that King Louis had not wished to give this great jewel, known as the 'Régale', to St Thomas's shrine, but it had flown from his hand and fastened itself to the tomb so that no one could move it.

In 1538, when King Henry VIII closed the monastery at Canterbury cathedral, he ordered the tomb to be destroyed. The jewels and the gold were put into huge chests and taken away by cart. No one knows where it all went, but the great ruby found its way into a ring, which Henry VIII wore on his thumb.